The *Common Sense* Mentor

For the

New Supervisor or Manager

By

John M. McClure

P.S. If you don't want to be a better manager or supervisor, don't bother to buy this book.

The *Common Sense* Mentor

ISBN: 979-8-218-06537-9 ebook
ISBN: 979-8-218-08566-7 Printed

Publisher: Mr. McMentor, LLC

Contact: info@mrmcmentor.com

3 - Table of Contents

1 - Title Page
2 - Copyright
3 - Table of Contents
4 – Preface   1
5 - About the Author   2
6 – Introduction   3
7 - New Supervisor or Manager   5
8 - Common Sense Manager Conduct   6
9 - Management 3-D Chess Game   8
10 – Planning   10
11 – Success and Failure Guidelines   11
12 - Types of Decisions   12
13 - Making A Decision   15
14 – Misinformation   18
15 - Sources of Confidential Information   19
16 - Predictable People   21
17 - Workplace Personalities   24
18 - Malicious Implementation   26
19 - Praise and Criticism   27
20 - Surviving A Crisis   29
21 - Hiring Relatives and Friends   30
22 - Management Workplace Friendships   32
23 - General Employee Meetings   35
24 - Individual Disciplinary Meetings   37
25 - Performance Review Meetings   38
26 - Written Communications   39
27 - Employee Appreciation   40
28 – Summary   41

4 - Preface

I wanted to create an easily referenced *common sense* support book for new supervisors and managers.

I wanted to cover basic subjects I have continually encountered during my 50 year career, 46 in management.

I wanted to help new managers become more aware of the types of business and employee issues they will experience during their new careers.

I wanted to give useful information which would help new managers use critical thinking and *common sense* in their new careers.

I wanted to help reduce their anxiety and stress in their new environment.

I wanted to help new managers become more successful.

I would like to acknowledge Sandra A. Zarcone, who assisted and counseled me while completing this book.

John M. McClure
September 2022

5 - About the Author

My 50 years in the paper distribution business started in 1964, in Washington State.

I was hired as a manual billing clerk, and in 1965, I was promoted to Customer Service, and then to Buyer/Merchandiser.

I was drafted for 2 years in 1966 and 1967.

I returned to my previous employer as Office Manager in 1968.

I retired from this company in 1997, after 33 years. During this time I had the following management titles beginning in 1968; Office Manager, Operations Manager, Merchandise Manager, Division Manager, Vice-President, and Sr. Vice-President.

During those 33 years, I had assignments in Alaska, Arizona, California, Colorado, Connecticut, Hawaii, Idaho, Massachusetts, Nevada, Utah, Vermont, and Washington

After retiring as a corporate soldier in 1997, I spent 17 years as an entrepreneur involved with companies in the paper, packaging, and food industries.

I made a lot of mistakes during my 50 year career, but I learned from every one of them. I hope this book helps you in your career.

6 - Introduction

It is a known fact the number 1 reason many employees leave their jobs is due to a bad "boss", not their job or the company.

What do employees want from supervisors or managers? What would a supervisor or manager want from employees? In my experience, as both an employee and a manager, it is fair to say all employees and managers want the same things.

Below is a list of characteristics and actions usually found in a successful and rewarding business environment. Are there any of these with which you disagree and think are not needed in your successful business environment?

- Respect
- Appreciation
- Recognition
- Integrity
- Consistency
- Training and Support
- Treated and talked to like an adult
- Opportunity to give opinions or input
- Knowledge of my job duties
- Be open to suggestions
- Use reasonable logic
- Demonstrate *COMMON SENSE*

We have a responsibility, as supervisors and managers, to ensure the stability and success of our business. We also have a responsibility to help our employees become successful.

The employees depend on us to make **good business decisions** in order for them to stay employed and continue to provide for their families.

This book is specifically designed for quick reference or refresher on a subject, in either an eBook or paperback format.

This book does not have all the answers, but hopefully, will stimulate your thought process, and open your mind to all the areas impacted in a business resulting from your actions.

Download the eBook to your phone, tablet, kindle, laptop, or desktop. Place the paperback copy of this book in your purse, your jacket, your back pocket, your briefcase, your desk, your backpack, or wherever keeps it handy.

Constantly use, reference, and review this book until it becomes mental muscle memory.

If you create a successful business environment, your employees will respond by making you successful.

7 - New Supervisor or Manager

What type of challenges do you face in your new position in a new department or company?

This book will try to give you relevant and common sense actions for these challenges.

Here are some general observation points you should be aware of in this new environment. Many of these points will be discussed later in this book.

- You have no established relationships
- You are not aware of the "pecking order" within this new environment
- You are not aware of who has the "political clout"
- Who are the "momentum control" people? (discussed later in book)
- Who is competent and who is not?
- Who can you trust?
- Listen, listen, and listen to what people have to say. It will help you evaluate employees later.
- Ask questions, questions, questions. The answers will help you evaluate employees later.
- Use your *common sense*.
- Employees will be watching to see how you measure up. Are you a competent or incompetent manager?

8 - *Common Sense* Manager Conduct

What is *common sense* professional management behavior?

It is simply performing your duties and responsibilities in a professional manner while respecting your employees and your company, and using *common sense*.

A manager demonstrating these positive actions listed below, consistently, will enjoy higher employee morale, and the employees' will have a higher opinion of you, as their manager.

Here are some general guidelines to help you become, and be acknowledged as a competent, *common sense*, and professional member of management.
- Keep confidential company information private.
- Be confident and professional when speaking with employees.
- Be on time to work, meetings, and appointments.
- Show respect when speaking to your employees.
- Show appreciation to your employees.
- Be neutral if asked about company politics.
- Dress professionally and appropriately for the business.
- Hold sensitive conversations in private.
- Discuss an employee's performance, both positive and negative, in private.
- Be timely with salary and benefit reviews, held in private, with your immediate employees.
- Be aware of the appearance of employee favoritism.
- Keep your personal financial information private.
- Be professional when socializing with employees.
- Be aware of your alcohol consumption around employees.
- Set boundaries when discussing your personal life with employees.

In other words, manage your employees as you would prefer to be managed.

Think, and use *common sense*, before you act.

Your employees will appreciate it, and they will also appreciate you so much more.

9 - Management's 3-D Chess Game
Think Beyond the Next Move

If you play chess, you understand that the strategy is to think several moves beyond your current move. Also, you need to have a general idea of where you are going and your strategy to get there.

Business is like a 3-D chess game, as you are vulnerable from every direction and plane.

Actions and reactions will bombard you from every direction; front, back, sides, diagonal, top, bottom, every angle.

In chess, you will sometimes see beginner players make a physical move on the board, but will not release their hold on the chess piece until, and after, spending time studying their exposure and vulnerability. More experienced players do this mentally before making a move.

When you are planning an action or making a decision, think beyond that initial step before acting. Ask yourself, what is going to be the reaction from employees, customers, vendors, or your boss?

Very few, if any, consistent chess winners blindly stumble through their games, not the least bit concerned about their next move.

Many managers do not think beyond the next move, decision or action. This is a big reason for so many confrontations, misunderstandings, and miscommunications in business.

This thought process and discipline, mixed with a little *common sense*, will reduce the surprises most managers face immediately after initiating an ill planned or ill prepared action.

9 - Management's 3-D Chess Game (cont'd)

Employees, who carry the brunt of management decisions, will appreciate the rarity of dealing with a competent, *common sense manager*, who actually thinks beyond the next move, and attempts to identify and anticipate the impact of their decisions on the business environment around them.

10 - Planning

Most plans succeed because they endure few changes to their original concept.

Conversely, most plans fail because of the constant changing the plan endures due to the obstacles and hurdles encountered in its implementation.

Most of these obstacles and hurdles should have been identified and addressed in the original plan preparation. If not, the original plan was conceived and implemented without a thorough analysis of issues.

A plan which succeeds is usually conceived by one person or a team. However, the plan should be analyzed and implemented by a team, not by an individual person.

A plan which is constantly changed, and therefore has little chance of success, is usually conceived by one person with power and authority, who does no logical *common sense* analysis, and insists the plan be implemented in an unreasonable length of time.

Make a plan. Work the plan. Overcome the obstacles. Don't change the plan.

11 - Success and Failure Guidelines

Plans, decisions, goals, objectives, and initiatives all have an equal chance of success or failure initially. If you would like to tip the balance in favor of either success or failure, use the following guidelines.

To improve your chances of success:
- Be sure the action is specific and measurable.
- Do not make frequent changes.
- Communicate clearly and frequently with the appropriate people.
- Strategize around the positive and negative impact of the action.
- Be aware of any potential disruption of working relationships (customer, vendor, sales, and employees).
- Do not arbitrarily change priorities.
- Make a plan, work the plan, overcome the obstacles, and don't change the plan. If the plan doesn't work, then change the plan.

To improve your chances of failure:
- Be sure the action is vague and no one can be held accountable.
- Make frequent changes.
- Communicate poorly, or not at all.
- Disregard the negative impact of the action.
- Disregard the disruption to working relationships impacted by the action.
- Arbitrarily and consistently change priorities.
- Don't make a plan, don't work the plan you don't have, be sure every obstacle to the plan you don't have stops your progress, and be sure to consistently change the plan you don't have. If the plan you don't have doesn't work, then don't make another plan.
- Full speed ahead.

11

12 - Types of Decisions

Early in my career, I may have read an article explaining the following types of decisions, and over the years I have put my own spin on them rating them 1 thru 10 with ten being the best decision.

All decisions made in the business environment fall into 5 categories. However, only 1 of these decisions is healthy for the business.

A basic understanding of these 5 categories allows for a quick analysis of the type of decision being made.

Being aware of and using this discipline, in a logical and consistent *common sense* manner, will allow you to realize whether you are involved with an *emotional, personal, political, bad business, or good business* decision.

Emotional Decision: The person making this decision disregards all other information and stimuli, and makes an *emotional decision* based upon their emotions at that moment. I rate this as a 1-2 on a scale of 10.

Example: A manager who goes critical, becomes angry, who performs or demands some type of action immediately.

Personal Decision: The person making this decision is disregarding all other information and stimuli, and is making a *personal decision* based only on what supports them personally, or their business agenda. I rate this as a 3-4 on a scale of 10.

Example: A manager disregarding a standing company policy in making a decision, as it would inconvenience a business associate.

12 - Types of Decisions (cont'd)

Political Decision: The person making this decision supports the position of another person or group in order to earn their favor. Everyone knows, including the decision maker, it was a *political decision*, and not the correct action. I rate this as a 5-6 on a scale of 10.

Example: A manager cancels a previous commitment to spend time and curry favor with a more senior manager which had not previously been scheduled.

Bad Business Decision: The person making this decision gathers all the information available, and attempts to make a good business decision, but makes a *bad business decision*. This decision will have some type of negative impact on the manager, the business, or both. I rate this as a 7-8 on a scale of 10, because they attempted to make a *good business decision*.

Example: A manager extending credit to an undeserving customer, and then taking an accounts receivable loss when the customer does not pay, or goes out of business.

Good Business Decision: The person making this decision listens, accumulates the necessary information, analyzes the options and alternatives, eliminates all the potential *emotional, personal, political, and bad business decisions,* and makes the *good business decision* that is healthy for the business.

Example: A manager who reviews the extension of credit to an undeserving customer, and makes the decision to not extend them any credit.

Generally, only the good business decision will nurture the business and employees, allowing both to grow over time.

12 - Types of Decisions (cont'd)

Emotional, personal, political, and bad business decisions will always erode the basic business foundation of the company and the morale of the employees. It may take a day, a week, a month, or years, but eventually, the company will pay dearly for allowing these types of decisions in their environment.

If you want to improve your skills as a competent, *common sense* manager, then you must constantly discipline yourself to always attempt to make the good business decision. Many managers will not.

We have all witnessed managers who have consistently made emotional, personal, political, or bad business decisions.

How did you feel when you witnessed those decisions?

Using the above logic and disciplines to make your decisions will help ensure other employees will see you as a competent *common sense* manager who consistently makes good business decisions.

Not all business decisions allow time for analysis. Many decisions are made in real time in business, and not all those real time decisions will be good business decisions.

During my career, I have made all 5 types of decisions on many occasions. However, I would reflect and learn from the effects of my decisions. I was determined to try and make the overwhelming majority of my decisions as good business decisions.

13 - Making A Decision

Do you promise to tell the truth, the whole truth, and nothing but the truth?

Most decisions are based upon information being received. The more accurate the information received, the better the odds of a more accurate *good business decision.*

People generally do not provide all the relevant information necessary to make a *good business decision.* It is our responsibility to seek out all the available information.

If we do not, then we will have been manipulated and victimized. If we make a quick decision, based only on what we are told, without the benefit of verification or questions, then it will usually be an *emotional decision* or a *bad business decision.*

One of the primary reasons people do not stop to seek the truth, it requires a conflict with the person they are conversing.

People do not like conflict. People are taught to be supportive of their family and friends. They are not taught to question their statements or actions.

To seek the truth requires a commitment of time and energy. Most people are unwilling to make this effort. It's too inconvenient. It's easier to accept what they are being told.

When employees approach a manager with issues they want resolved or directions on their next step, the manager has a tendency to respond immediately.

Managers think they need to be all knowing and powerful, like the professor in the "Wizard of Oz".

13 - Making A Decision (cont'd)

The first thing a manager needs to do is listen. The second thing is to not talk and continue listening. The third, fourth, and fifth are to be alert, be cautious, and ask questions, lots of questions.

Take your time. Ask more questions. This will help you unravel and understand more of the facts of the actual situation.

This, in turn, will help you visualize and comprehend the larger implications and results of your response to the employee.

If, after making your initial good business decision, additional facts are revealed which alters the situation, then the competent, common sense manager, has the right and responsibility to alter his original decision and make a better good business decision.

New managers are quickly categorized and manipulated by their employees. They will know your strengths and weaknesses from your demonstrated decision making skills.

Employees consider most managers incompetent. Their assumptions are quickly validated as they observe their incompetent manager's daily and predictable emotional, personal, political, and bad business decisions.

Based on these observations, the employees will adjust their approach to play to the manager's weaknesses, and manipulate the manager's decisions without the incompetent manager being the wiser.

The manager will feel "in-charge" because they made a decision, and the employee will feel "in-charge" because they got what they wanted.

13 - Making A Decision (cont'd)

The employees will see you consistently being manipulated, and lose confidence in your ability to manage effectively.

This environment will contribute to employee issues and employee turnover.

Both competent and incompetent employees will respect a competent manager.

All employees will see the competent, *common sense manager* consistently resist the urge to make emotional, personal, political, and bad business decisions.

The competent *common sense manager* will be consistent and dependable in their attempts to make good business decisions.

This consistency and dependability helps stabilize the work force, and has a positive impact on employee morale.

Not many people realize or recognize that employees actually run their companies, not the management. Employees perform the daily functions of every company, which allows the company to function.

Our job, as supervisors and managers, is to lead and communicate where we are going, and how we are going to get there.

Learn what your employees are doing each day, each week. What deadlines do they need to meet? What are the hurdles and obstacles they face and must overcome to complete their jobs? What do they stress over?

Learn to appreciate your employees, and they will learn to appreciate their manager.

14 - Misinformation

Misinformation, rumors, and whispers are toxic for a business environment, especially to the employees.

This misinformation, unchallenged, will lead to management potentially making personal, emotional, political, or bad business decisions.

Continually acting on misinformation will lead to low morale, productivity loss, employee turnover, and reinforce the general mistrust of management.

Misinformation creates communication issues, and paints inaccurate assessments of people, actions, and processes.

Incompetent managers pass on this misinformation, without challenging or confirming the info, and because of their position, will expect it to be acted upon by their subordinates.

You need to challenge verbal information until you reach a comfort level in its accuracy.

Learn to stop it. Do not be a victim. Use *common sense*.

15 - Sources of Confidential Information

How is confidential information obtained by individuals in your business environment? Usually by overhearing conversations or being exposed to written confidential information.

Unknowingly, you could expose confidential information in your personal office or work area to visitors, vendors, or employees as they are talking or meeting with you. Open files, miscellaneous documents, or an unattended computer screen could expose this restricted information.

When a visitor, vendor, or employee enters your office or work area, watch their actions. Do they seem distracted as they scan the area? Do they begin touching and moving papers and files?

Do they immediately begin asking questions regarding something they saw in your work area? Are they looking directly at you or busy scanning your desk or work area?

I am not suggestion you become paranoid about protecting confidential information located in your office or work area. What I am suggesting is for you to be alert, be aware, and use *common sense*. Don't be a victim.

If you feel compromised by a visitor or employee, immediately challenge them in a firm, but professional manner.

Communicate to them that their behavior is unappreciated, inappropriate, and unacceptable.

Let them know in the future you expect them to behave in a more respectful and professional manner.

However, before they leave your office, make sure they understand they are still welcome in your office. You do not want people to be afraid to visit your office or work area.

Do not allow yourself to be victimized. Stay alert. Be competent. Use *common sense*.

16 - Predictable People

Most people are predictable. Given a specific set of circumstances, they will behave in a consistently predictable manner. We all have family members or friends who are perfect examples of this behavior.

If you take the time to learn what values and motivations your employees are about, you will begin predicting their behavior in given situations.

There are several ways to develop this skill. Observe and interact with the individuals to learn their values, standards, commitment, determination, motivation, and the processes used, or lack thereof, to analyze situations.

Observe their behavior during meetings. Who do they associate with? Are they strong or weak to outside influences? Do they use *common sense* or are they *emotional*?

How do they handle *political* pressure? Are they rational or incoherent under pressure? Do they meet deadlines?

Being able to predict behavior is a valuable discipline to develop and use as a manager. If used with *common sense*, it can help you be seen by your employees as a competent *common sense* manager.

When manager's receive information, they usually think they are faced with 2 simple choices, believe the information or don't believe it. Those would be the simple conclusions relied upon by most managers.

However, based upon your knowledge of the predictable behavior of the individuals involved, your gut will tell you if the information is not credible, partially credible, or entirely credible. You then can confidently take whatever actions you deem necessary.

16 - Predictable People (cont'd)

Using the *common sense* approach to dealing with predictable people should actually take less time than an emotional approach.

Here are the actions of an incompetent manager acting on misinformation.

1. The manager believed the information was correct, took immediate action, but later found the information to be incorrect.
2. The manager believed the information was incorrect, took immediate action, but later found the information to be correct.

The consequences of the above actions are as follows:

1. Verification to your employees that you are a member of the incompetent manager group.
2. The employee, who conveyed the misinformation, now knows you can be manipulated.
3. You should realize you were used, abused, and victimized.
4. The wrongly accused, if an employee, will feel betrayed by you.

Using the competent *common sense* manager predictable people approach to acting on misinformation has the following results.

1. You verified the actual facts.
2. You were not manipulated.
3. You were not victimized.
4. The company was not victimized.
5. The employees will have a new appreciation and respect for you and your *common sense* management style.

16 - Predictable People (cont'd)

The best defense is a good offense. These are people we deal with who are generally emotional, and have little facts to support their position.

However, they will become much louder in the conversation, if they feel they are not winning their point.

They will begin to bring into the conversation vague issues, past situations, other employee examples. Anything and everything that cannot be verified, and is irrelevant, will be thrown at you.

This all because they can't substantiate their position, but are determined to win.

You must not get emotional, or you will lose. You must be strong and consistent. If you have confidence in your facts, do not do more work to try and convince this person of your position.

These types of people can be very time consuming for you, if you do not recognize this type of behavior.

They will reduce your productivity and potentially cause morale problems in your department.

17 - Workplace Personalities

In each office there are employees who actually have more impact on your personal success, or the company's, than most people can imagine.

We call them the "momentum control" employee and they are generally not the person in charge.

Many beneficial actions or programs introduced by management which fail or achieve disappointing results, can be attributed to these people. Most managers will not pick up on this obstruction.

When a program fails due to these employees, some managers may simply scratch their heads, and make a new plan and try their luck again.

The competent *common sense* manager will investigate the obstruction, and probably identify the "momentum control" person.

This person is generally a long term employee with a strong personality. There are 2 types. One is incompetent and they do a lot of damage. The other is a conscientious employee who cares about the company, and is trying to protect the company from incompetent managers' activities doing damage to the company.

When new programs, policies, procedures, strategies, social functions, promotions, demotions are announced, the employees will look to the "momentum control" person for their reaction. This is all done covertly.

The "momentum control" person will decide whether it is good or bad for the employees or company, or if it is beneficial and to what extent it should be supported.

If you can identify this employee, and you determine they are not malicious, then this is the person you want to win over.

Communicate with them; discuss thoughts and ideas with them. If you can convince them that you are a *common sense* logical manager, they can become your biggest supporter, and ensure your programs are accepted by the other employees.

Use your predictable people skills to identify this individual. They are not hard to find, but you have to be aware of what you are looking for.

This is predictable behavior. There is no need for stress, frustration, or panic when facing this situation. Simply continue to apply consistent, competent, *common sense*, and good business decision analysis.

The malicious "momentum control" person is very dangerous. Depending on their attitude and the severity of the problems created, they need to be disciplined up to and including discharge.

The protective "momentum control" person can help you have a very positive effect on your business.

Also, be aware of the "rock throwers". They are employees who are always suggesting you look over there, if there is a problem. Do not look at me.

They are usually trying to divert your attention from themselves, or hide their incompetency.

A statement I read early in my career, and have used many times during my career is as follows, "incompetent people cannot survive in a competent environment, and competent people cannot survive in an incompetent environment."

18 - Malicious Implementation

In some companies, we find employees who will purposely sabotage old or new processes and procedures.

This employee is different than the "momentum control" employee. This person is more subtle, and more difficult to identify.

This may be an employee who makes a lot of mistakes, or is always late to work, or misses deadlines.

The employee liked a process or procedure which was replaced with a new process or procedure. They then bastardize the new process to make it more like the old process as an act of rebellion against change.

This person will not have a positive attitude, and may not be salvageable.

19 - Praise and Criticism

You should only accept praise and criticism from people you respect. This is the only praise or criticism that should earn your attention and energy.

Reflecting on the opinions of people you respect, who critique your actions, will result in a long term, healthy growth of a realistic *common sense* management style.

Do not accept praise or criticism from people you do not respect. It is important to discipline yourself to understand this difference.

Many incompetent managers will waste valuable time and energy on the generous, but erroneous, observations of people who don't deserve that effort.

Common sense dictates we have only so much time and energy to expend each day as managers, so we should make it count.

Pay attention only to people who truly care about your personal and professional growth. They will be the people you respect.

All others will be phony and will probably have an ulterior motive. Their praise of you probably will be politically motivated.

Their criticism probably will be due to jealousy, ignorance, or *misinformation*.

Their criticism may also be due to basic incompetence, or they may embrace a peculiar satisfaction in putting you, or anyone else, down.

Whatever the issue, do not waste your valuable time stressing over the praise or criticism of people you do not respect. Use your common sense and reasoning, along with awareness and discipline, to protect your emotions from being manipulated.

19 - Praise and Criticism (cont'd)

Do not change who you are, or what you believe in.

People you respect, whose praise and criticism you accept, will also share advice, alternatives, options, and alternate solutions with you.

They will be your mentors.

They will be your coaches.

They will care about your professional and personal growth and success.

In return, this is what a competent *common sense* manager should be to their employees.

20 - Surviving A Crisis

Unfortunately, we will all experience personal and professional crises during our lifetime. It is part of life.

Mentally speaking, you will survive any crisis. It is only a question of who you will be when you emerge on the other side and the crisis has passed.

Have you grown from the experience? Were you calm or did you panic? Are you a wiser person? Have you learned anything from the experience?

If faced with this type of crisis again, will you be any better prepared to see it through? Can you apply any learned skills from one crisis to the next?

With experience and awareness, it is possible to anticipate future crises. Therefore you can take steps to reduce or eliminate them and the stress associated with them.

Applying learned experiences may allow you to reduce the cost of resolving the next crisis, or save an employee from leaving, or save a customer or vendor, or turn defeat into victory.

You will have demonstrated your level headedness as a competent *common sense* manager.

You can learn as much, or more, from the unsuccessful resolution of a crisis, as you can from the successful resolution of a crisis.

To meet your objective of being known as a member of that elite, but small group known as competent *common sense* managers, you must learn and grow from each experience. You must apply this knowledge to the next opportunity.

Remember, a crisis is an opportunity for you to demonstrate your *common sense* managerial and leadership skills.

21 - Hiring Friends and Relatives

When you have a job opening and need to hire a new employee, often a current employee will recommend a close relative or friend.

It is a quick way to fill a position without the hassle of placing ads and interviewing people.

If you hire a friend or relative, it is almost always done with less vetting than you would do with a regular applicant.

After you hire a friend or relative of a current employee, work will go well, until it doesn't go well.

Then, if you have a problem with the employee, or the employee's friend or relative, you will most likely have a problem with both employees.

If you have issues or problems, it is human nature to seek counsel, support, and sympathy from family or friends, or possibly other employees.

Few people are strong enough and have enough *common sense* to maintain a strong and stable relationship, and also be objective during emotional times.

Therefore, if you have a disciplinary or performance problem with one of these employees, you will most likely be dealing with multiple employee issues through to its resolution.

This is an absolutely predictable situation. You witness it every day in your personal life in the interaction between your family, relatives, or friends.

It is also part of the business environment. It is not something to stress over.

When you analyze the employee issue and potential solutions, this is simply one of the strategies that must be thought through.

21 - Hiring Friends and Relatives (cont'd)

In no case do you shy away from the problem due to these types of circumstances. Your responsibility, as a competent *common sense* manager, is to address the issue and resolve it with your best good business decision.

22 - Management Workplace Friendships

What is friendship? The measurement of a true friend is not in the easy, unchallenging, non-committal actions they share with us on a daily basis. It is the hard, only occasional, extremely challenging, get-in-the-game, major crisis that drops on us unexpectedly.

Friends may not agree with your words or actions, but they will give you consistent support and advice.

Friends consistently do not take advantage of you.

Can you be a consistent common sense manager and be friends with an employee?

"Your friendship will be strong, if you are a good leader. Your leadership will be weak, if you are a good friend."

We want to remain accessible to employees. However, the employees must always know you are their manager first and foremost.

They have to be gently reminded, in the event they ask questions which are inappropriate or require the disclosure of confidential information, the relationship does not allow for that type of information exchange.

Reinforce to them they need to respect your position and responsibilities first, or there can be no friendship outside of business.

Employees cannot be allowed to abuse their relationship with you, as a manager, to obtain knowledge they normally would not have access to.

Other employees are constantly monitoring your behavior. If they conclude you are sharing confidential or "inside information" with your "friends", you will have employee morale, performance, and motivational problems with them.

Employees will begin to withdraw from contact with you. They will feel you cannot be trusted with new or old information previously shared with you.

They will feel violated.

This is all minimized if you use consistent, logical, common sense, and a good business decision thought process when dealing with your employees.

It is also common for employees to try to obtain confidential or "insider" information from you without the guise of "friendship".

If the employee is successful, it is often used to increase their influence over others, or their perceived standing in the company's "pecking order'.

Employees have an insatiable thirst for this kind of "forbidden knowledge". They seek out, and even revere, those employees who always seem to possess some "forbidden knowledge" information.

It never really matters whether it is true or false, and rarely is the effort made to verify its truthfulness. It is simply assumed to be true, and the office rumor mill is immediately put into motion to do its damage.

Obviously, this issue costs the company in many ways. Lost productivity, employee morale problems, employee turnover, compensation issues, and wasted management time addressing the issues.

Be alert. Be aware. Be consistent. Use *common sense.*

Be careful of what you say, where you say it, and to what audience you say it.

22 - Management Workplace Friendships (cont'd)

Competent managers are consistently aware of the balance needed to maintain a healthy relationship between managers and their employees.

23 - General Employee Meetings

General employee meetings can be tailored to different groups such as all employees, salespeople only, customer service employees, office, credit, warehouse, or delivery. Any combination you deem necessary.

Each meeting should have a few items in common.

Prepare for the meeting. Don't wing it.
- Review your objectives for the meeting. What are you trying to accomplish?
- Have a written agenda.
- Set a specific time for the meeting.
- Set a specific length of time for the meeting.
- Give as much advance notice as possible to the employee group.
- Be aware of each group's daily priorities and try not to schedule meetings that interrupt that time period.
- Try to use humor and creativity, if it is appropriate, during your meeting. This will be determined by the purpose of the meeting. Is it a general meeting or a serious meeting?
- Communicate openly. There are 3 comments you should make at the beginning of the meeting regarding answering questions.
  - I'll answer the question to the best of my knowledge.
  - I'll admit I don't know the answer, but will get the answer and respond back to you.
  - I know the answer, but it is confidential, and I can't share it with you.
- Your general comments can include information about future company or department plans.
- Positive comments about the company and specific employee group or department in the meeting.

35

23- General Employee Meetings (cont'd)

- Keep your comments real and positive, even if you are in the middle of a crisis.
- The employees need to see you as a confident leader when the meeting is over.

24 - Individual Disciplinary Meeting

An individual disciplinary meeting should be scheduled as quickly after an incident as possible without disrupting the business.

Here are some bullet point suggestions to use during this type of employee meeting.

- Set a firm time commitment for the meeting. Do not allow the employee to extend the meeting beyond this set period of time.
- Ask the employee to explain their actions.
- Ask direct questions regarding the incident.
- Wait for the employee to answer your question, do not answer for them.
- Try not to ask questions which can be answered with a yes or no.
- Ask how they might handle the same situation differently in the future.
- Quote or reference company policies, rules, or procedures that apply to the situation.
- Do not be cornered into justifying the company's position.
- State "if this behavior continues, there will be additional disciplinary action up to an including discharge".

25 - Performance Review Meetings

Performance review meetings should be held with each employee at least once a year, or more frequently if there is a company policy.

If your company has a review/performance form, have the employee complete it before your scheduled review meeting, and forward it to you for review ahead of the sit down review with the employee.

Schedule the review at a time when it will not conflict with their duties. You want the employee to be focused on the review, and not on the work still to be done on their desk.

Let the employee talk. You listen.

Keep the review focused on the employee's strengths and weaknesses. Make a plan with the employee's input to help improve any skills they are lacking.

Be professional, be positive, be supportive, but be honest about your praise or criticism.

If the employee is to get a raise, tell them the new monthly salary or hourly rate, and the effective date.

Let them ask questions, but do not allow the meeting to go beyond your allotted time.

26 - Written Communications

As a manager or supervisor, you will need to communicate in writing for various reasons.

The communications could be to your group of employees, or to other groups. They may be formal or informal. They could be to vendors, customers, or your boss.

Items to consider in your communications:
- What are you trying to communicate?
- The format
- Be specific
- Be professional
- Be concise
- Remove any emotion, just facts
- Try not to be negative
- Write clearly, so the message is received
- Quote company policies or procedures, if needed
- Decide who to copy and why
- List your copied recipients so all will know who received the memo.
- Use spell check
- Edit, edit, edit

27 - Employee Appreciation

Employees welcome company sponsored activities as it communicates to them they are important and appreciated.

Here are suggestions for company sponsored activities which show employee appreciation and has the added benefit of creating team spirit. Have fun. Be creative.

- Office luncheons
- Pot Luck
- Christmas Party
- Halloween office party
- Afternoon snacks
- Company picnic
- Company Bar-B-Q
- Theme lunches
- Recognition ceremonies
- Company sports team
- Logo items such as shirts, hats, pens

Examples of an afternoon holiday function for Cinco de Mayo.

- Use break room or lunchroom
- Serve miniature tacos
- Chips and salsa
- Water and sodas

Always remind the employees about safety during activities and safe driving after the activities.

28 - Summary

Think of this book as your mentor. This is the advice and coaching I would give you on your journey to become a successful *common sense* supervisor or manager.

When you have questions, or doubts, or you are unsure, or just want advice, reference this book and see if there is something in here that may help you, before going into your own boss for the answer or advice.

Wouldn't you feel more confident if you were able to tell your boss how you solved or resolved an issue?

As a new supervisor or manager, you are the future of the company. You will inherit more and more responsibility as time goes on. Be prepared, as it will happen.

Always remember the employees know how to run the business, our job is not to put obstacles in their path, but appreciate and respect them.

Our job is to give them leadership and direction, and *common sense* management.

Notes

<u>Notes</u>

Notes

Made in the USA
Middletown, DE
13 February 2023

24829740R00029